The Anger Inside

Copyright May 2022 Michelle Clayton
Published by Green Heart Living Press

Layout and Typesetting: Hattice Bayramoglu

Illustrations: Hattice Bayramoglu

ISBN: 978-1-95-449325-4

All rights reserved.

It is not legal to reproduce, duplicate, or transmit any part of this document in either electronic means or printed format.

Recording of this publication is strictly prohibited.

To contact the publisher, please visit
WWW.GrowWithMJC.com

This book is dedicated to
Brooke and D'Andre.

Tough things will happen, but my
greatest wish is for you
to feel life fully,
to know you are worthy,
and to know that your feelings
are valid.

I love you so much.

Mom

The Anger Inside

Written by: Michelle Clayton
Illustrated by Hatice Bayramoglu

Hi! My name is Anger E. Motion!
I am an emotion. It's nice to meet you.
What's your name?

I'm glad to get to know you because some people are afraid of me, but only because they don't understand me.

I am a protector emotion.
I protect and hide my friends.

Here are some of my friends:

Sadness E. Motion

Fear E. Motion

Helplessness E. Motion

Pain E. Motion

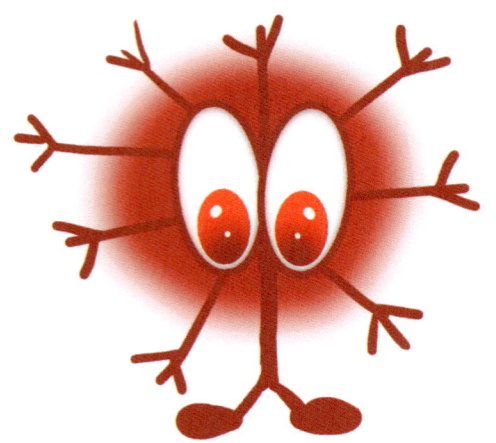

Have you ever felt like someone is squeezing your chest?

Have you felt your face and ears get hot?

Have you made fists with your hands?

Have you felt your jaw get tight?

How do you feel when I am in your body?

Can you show me where you feel anger inside your body?

When I show up inside your body It is OKAY!
It does NOT mean you are bad.

I am here to help!
I'm sending you a message.

Anger is a human emotion that EVERYONE feels.

**Anger is NOT bad.
You getting angry is NOT a bad thing.**

There are things it is not okay to USE me for:

Do not USE me to hit ANYONE.

Do not USE me to break things.

Do not USE me to hurt others.

Do not USE me to say mean things.

THAT is NOT what I am here for.

I am here to HELP you!

Here are some things I can help you do:

Speak up for yourself.
Say "NO!"
Be brave when you are scared.
Stick up for others.

I am here to SHOW you where you WANT to create change. I am here to help, then leave.

I am not meant to be with you all the time.
I like to do my own thing!

Your job is to feel me, then let me go.
My job is to help you find my friend that is hiding while I was with you.
What can you do to let me go?

I like it best when people help me leave by:

**What is your favorite way?
Draw a picture showing your favorite way
to help anger leave.**

I want you to know that it is important to get to know me and why I came to protect my friend. You have to let me go to feel what I am hiding.

You ARE important!
How you feel is important too!

It was nice to meet you,
but it is time for me to leave.

Deep breath in...

Deep breath out.

The end...for now...

Color me!

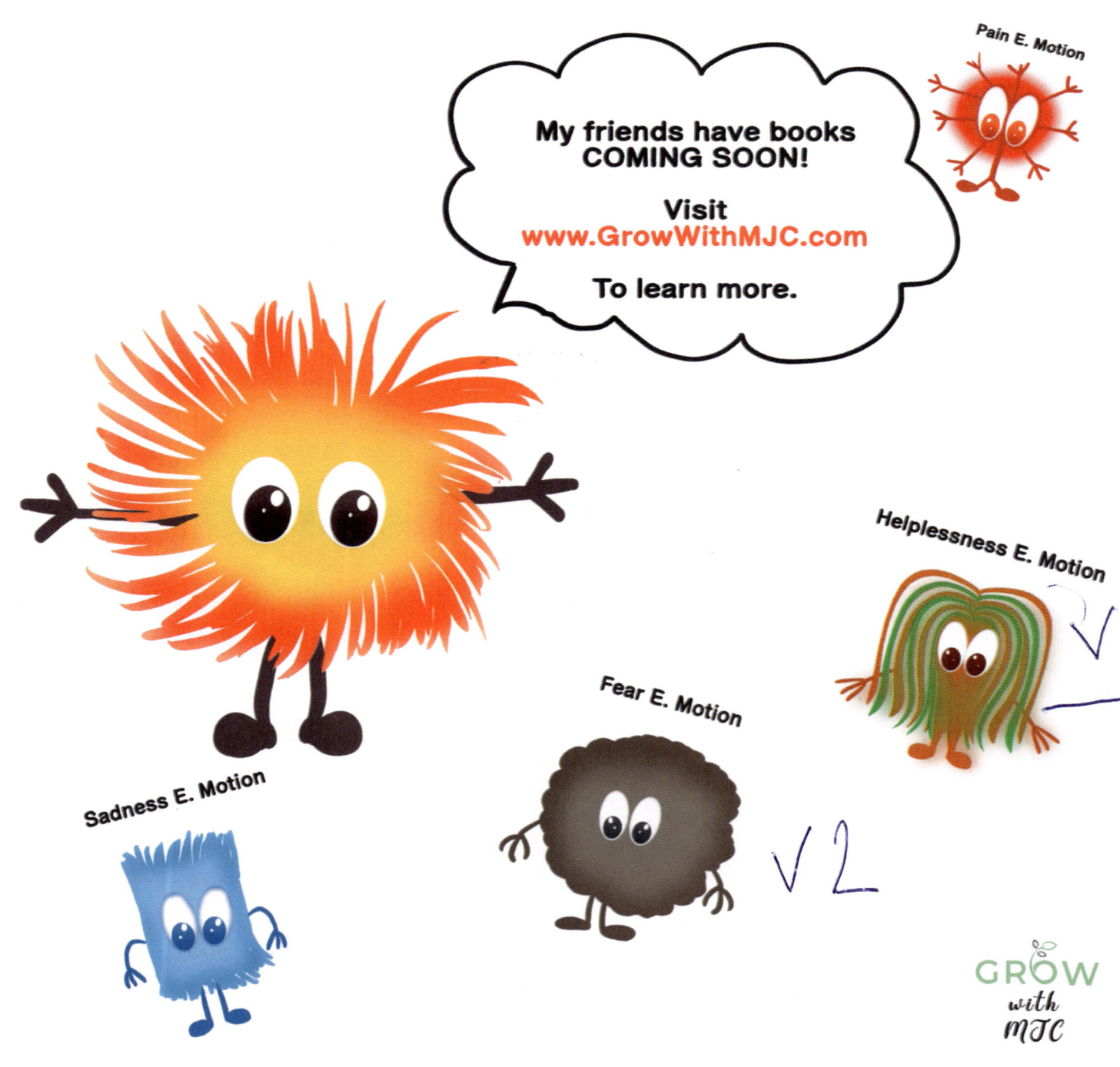

Printed in Great Britain
by Amazon